SANTA IS A SLUT

DREA DENAE

Cover Design: Nikki Epperson

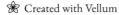 Created with Vellum

For my dirty little elves.

Sit on whatever laps you want to (with their consent).

Love whoever you want to.

Read whateverthefuck you want to.

Be nice or be naughty.

And if they tell you to be quiet, yell louder.

author's note

This is a novella, which is defined as a long short story. I would like to make it clear, this is NOT a full-length book.

If you are looking for a story with intricate emotional plot lines and intense character development, this is not the story for you right now.

If you are looking for a short story high in smut, puns, and cliches centered around the Christmas season, I HAVE EXCELLENT NEWS.

Santa Is A Slut is a why choose, polyamorous romance. Every main character in this story is going to bang. I'm certain the side characters are also getting laid if they wish...but this isn't about them. Is everything going to make sense? No, baby girl, because it's riDICKulous fiction.

Hold on to your panties or let them fly right off, this ride is fast-paced and there is the potential you might get wet.

While it is the second book in the Holiday Hoemies series, it is an interconnected story and therefore not necessary to read Cupid first.

There are explicit scenes with MM, FF, MMF, FFM, and FFMM relationships. These scenes may include things like squirting, degradation, anal play, oral sex, toys, spanking and a lot of orgasms.

Potential triggers: hidden agenda, light angst, a little miscommunication

"*W*hat do you mean you're moving?" I ask incredulously. Surely, this woman is playing a twisted joke.

Val sighs before giving me a sympathetic look. "Noel, I'll still be in the same city as you and we'll see each other all the time."

I see she's made the decision to pacify me with classic lies. Crossing my arms over my chest, I pout and mumble under my breath, "Not as much as you see dick."

My best friend is abandoning me for her hot bosses turned boyfriends turned freaking co-inhabitants. I should have known something was up when she suggested we camp out in the living room last night to watch my favorite movies. I should have suspected bad news when she brought out the cupcakes I like from the bakery across town. And I really should have guessed she was preparing me for bad news when I woke up to the phallic-shaped donuts that she had delivered for breakfast.

I knew it was coming. Val has been dating Beau, Hart, and Romeo for almost a year. I've been waiting for them to ask me to help them pick a ring; I should have been preparing for them to steal her away for good.

Assholes.

"One more year. We can make a roomie bucket list and check things off super slowly and appreciate the deep friendship we've forged." I'm bargaining with desperation despite knowing it's a lost cause.

Val wraps her arms around me. "You're my best friend. You'll always be my best friend, no matter how far away I live. Luckily, I'll be close by so we can still make that list. Just go ahead and cross off any orgies or sex dungeons."

She's trying to ruin all the fun today.

I don't understand why she's making me eliminate the best ideas considering she is pretty much the orgy queen, taking three dicks on the regular. But whatever. Some girls have all the luck.

"Fine. I guess you can go live with all your boyfriends and just leave me here to die alone. I'll make sure to adopt some cats that will be kind enough to feed from my remains when I succumb to mortality since I'm sure you'll still be too busy having loads of sex to check on me."

If she was thinking I would be reasonable about this, she is dead wrong. I've never been even a little reasonable in my entire life and I'm not going to waste a chance to be as dramatic as possible, hoping that she'll feel guilty enough to change her mind.

It's a lost cause because all she does is laugh. "I'm sure I'll continue having stupid amounts of sex with mind-blowing orgasms but I'll always make time for you, Noel. Would you like to continue in this pit of despair you're digging or bitch about your boss until I have to leave?"

Val is good. As good as option number one sounds, she knows I can't resist option two.

Ever since Scrooge McDoucheFace, also known as Nicholas, took over Santaland, we've put up with change after change. None of them are good changes either.

I've made sure to complain about him regularly to Val. A girl has to vent to her best friend so she can avoid turning her workplace into a rage room. Every time a new employee memo comes out, I think about grabbing a giant fake candy cane and shoving it up Nicholas's ass.

"You've got that look on your face that normally ends in trouble. What's going on now?" Val asks.

"Nothing new but I'm certain that will change by the time I make it into work. I was just imagining my new boss taking a candy cane up the ass courtesy of me." It's a nice fantasy. Maybe I'll draw it out stick figure style and frame it.

"Lube or no lube?" she asks with a raised brow.

"I'd make an exception to my policy for him."

"No lube, no back tube," we say in unison. I've been preaching it since our college days. "I could maybe spit on it, even though it's not a sufficient replacement. If I was feeling charitable."

Val laughs and I can't help but smile.

I know I'll still see her, realistically, but we've lived together for so much of our lives that this feels like a very serious change. It scares me and she knows it.

Drea Denae

"I'm going to miss you, Val. So much. I am happy for you and I know those assholes love you. They'll take care of you. But I'll miss you." I hold back the tears that are begging to fall.

She wraps me in another hug and I embrace her back. "I'll miss you too, Noel."

We spend the rest of our time in comfortable silence but I can't help but wonder how much lonelier I'm going to feel once her things disappear from our apartment.

I don't want to be alone.

* * *

WHAT. A. Fucking. Twat.

An absolute asshole.

The most massive fuckwad in all of tarnation. Or at least in SantaScape.

I crumble up the newest employee memo and throw it on the ground before promptly picking it right back up and finding the nearest recycle bin.

Val would be mortified if she knew I was contemplating littering considering that she works for the sustainability company that her three boyfriends all own.

Remembering how Val and said hot boyfriends broke my heart this morning, I almost retrieve the tossed paper and throw it back on the floor.

Of course, the shitty day couldn't just end there. Nope.

Not with Mr. Scroogy McSnooze in town.

Sweet old Santa left us last year. Not like...left us as in he died. Mr. Bates just abandoned us for the Bahamas and is living his best retirement life with his wife Carol.

His nephew, Nicholas, is the exact opposite of what anyone would expect from the new "Christmas King". Since he started, the guy has sent out at least one work memo a day changing the many traditions of SantaScape.

First, no more after party. We're just expected to work ourselves to the bone every single day with no celebration at the end of the season.

Then there were the costume changes. Before, we had modern adorable themed outfits with striped leggings and fitted attire. Now we look like an elf fucked a present box. I'm a walking gift with ears.

Now, he has the audacity to give us a script to follow, ensuring each child that comes to make a wish to Santa only has two minutes to do so.

Santa fright is a real thing. Some kids take two minutes just to muster up the word "hi".

I was bummed when all of the changes affected me and my daily routine but now that he's messing with the kids...these itchy green gloves are coming off.

Well, figuratively...for now.

I hold my head high as I march my way to the office of my target. I'm ready to be fired. I'm ready for any consequences. I am ready to unleash every bit of rage I've contained inside my body for this.

Nicholas, watch out.

Instead of barging in, I pause outside the entry to his office. I need a few minutes to calm myself down first. After all, I still have a secretary to trick into letting me barge into our boss's office without an appointment. There's no way I'm going to fool her if I walk in looking like an elf from a gory horror film.

Only, there's no one at the desk to stop me. It's a little early in the day for a lunch break but I'm not going to dwell on it.

two

I don't often spend my lunch hour fucking my secretary's face but sometimes it's the only thing that stops me from trying to sell this place for parts.

Besides, Eve has been one of two reasons I've even enjoyed showing up to my office. Well, technically there are three but I like to pretend that the third one doesn't exist.

Reason number two is currently licking reason number one's sweet little pussy.

As a general rule, I don't usually fuck around with my staff but I'm only here as their boss temporarily. My younger brother, Jack, is planning to take over SantaScape after this holiday season. He was supposed to be here already but apparently he ran into some crisis over Halloween weekend that has him completely unavailable.

Though I have no regrets seeing Eve splayed out on my desk with Kane at the other end with his head between her legs.

Eve senses my distraction and decides to try and put on a show for me. She lifts her hips and puts one hand on the back of Kane's head, forcing his mouth to her clit. Her other hand comes up and grips my balls.

"Unless you want to suck on those, you better focus on swallowing my cock until my cum floods that naughty little mouth."

Her eyes roll back into her head at my words and Kane chuckles against her.

"If you can laugh, you're probably eating that pussy like a lost little school boy. Be a fucking man and drown in her cunt or I'll spank your ass so hard you won't be able to sit down until the New Year."

Kane immediately rises to the challenge. Eating Eve out like he's been missing every meal for a month and she's the only thing saving him from starvation.

I try to lose myself in the sensation of a beautiful woman gagging on my cock, feeling how wet and tight her throat feels. I think about how tomorrow I'm going to make Kane eat her pussy again but I'll be behind him, fucking his ass while I taunt him.

Eve moans around me, signaling that she's close, and the vibration is almost enough to have me letting go. I think about whether I would rather paint her tits with my cum so Kane can clean it off or make her swallow it and have Kane lick me clean.

The choice is made for me when reason number three shoves my office door open.

Meeting the fiery little elf's eyes, my orgasm builds in my spine and sends a shock through me. I barely give Eve a grunt in warning before I fill her mouth with one last rough thrust, holding myself in her throat until I'm spent.

If Noel is shocked, she quickly hides it. She smirks as if she thinks walking in at this moment somehow gives her an upper hand.

Eve moans loudly, drawing my attention back to my lunch dates. Kane looks up with his mouth glistening, proud of himself but torn over what to do now.

When Eve attempts to scramble up and off of my desk, I grab her by the throat to hold her in place.

"Did I give you permission to leave?"

She shakes her head before looking towards the door. I turn her back to me, unwilling to let her or Kane give in to this distraction.

"You've both made a mess. On my desk and on my dick. Clean it up," I command.

Neither of them move.

I look at Noel and sigh. "You can watch but if these two don't follow my orders, I'll be spending the lunch hour tomorrow edging them until they can't remember their names."

Noel lets out a laugh when both Kane and Eve move quickly to avoid that punishment. They're aware of exactly how much pleasure I can torture them with and neither of them are willing to risk that fate.

"Shame. Sounds like you could have punished them and I could have taken them both to the storage closet on the second floor to give them the desperate relief they need." She shrugs.

That smirk is still on her face, telling me that she most likely has her own history with these two. Which only heightens my lust for the three of them. The only jealousy I feel is over the fact that I might be missing out on their playtime.

"How can I help you, Noel? Clearly, you must have something urgent to discuss if you're willing to interrupt my private lunch hour." I infuse as much anger as I can muster into my voice, which proves to be difficult as Kane and Eve begin to take turns licking my cock clean.

"Do you mean private *hump* hour?" Noel giggles at her joke, impressed by her own humor.

"If you have nothing to discuss then it's best you go," I say dismissively. Even though I love seeing the way she's trying to fight the instinct to look down.

"Nothing to discuss?" Noel's voice escalates. "Where should I even start, you maniacal jackass?"

If her voice gets any higher, I'm pretty sure she'll be screeching. It's also really hard to take her seriously when she's caught me with my pants down.

Literally.

"Name calling is a little immature, wouldn't you say so?" I ask the room, looking for Eve or Kane to back me up.

The two of them are too busy tugging their clothes back on at a leisurely pace to weigh in right away. They seem unbothered by our intruder, so I can only guess I should follow their lead.

Eve shrugs once she's dressed, "Maybe it's immature, but she's not wrong."

The little vixen gives Noel a wink.

Kane just laughs as if this entire situation is absurd.

"You continue to ruin this place, dragging everything into the ground, pretending like you're too good for SantaScape while sit up here in your office, completely uncaring of its demise," Noel seethes.

She walks further into the office, approaching my desk with her hands in fists at her sides.

I'm impressed and annoyed by her dramatic flair. Little does she know that every single change I've made is in the hope that I can keep this place going long enough to hand it over at the end of the year. However, I feel no need to explain myself.

"Listen to me, little elf. You entered *my* office without permission. You come in here with your accusations and name calling like this isn't a professional setting." My voice is steady but I don't hide the genuine anger in my harsh tone.

The air in the room changes from playful to dangerous as I roll my shoulders back. The mood shifts and I watch as Kane and Eve quickly excuse themselves without a word.

Noel allows them past her at the door and I watch as she gulps nervously, losing just a little of that fire she walked in here with.

I place my hands on my desk and lean forward in a way that I know looks intimidating. Then I continue, "But this *is* a professional setting. This is a job and if you don't like it, you can leave. Everything here will still happen, with or without you. So either get with it or get the fuck out."

Noel's eyes widen before quickly narrowing into angry slits. "You're not going to scare me out of here. You're going to stop making all of these shitty changes and pissing off your employees."

"Or what?" I ask, raising a brow. "You'll all quit?"

She crosses her arms and lifts a shoulder.

"Try it," I say with a mocking laugh. "Seasonal work is easily filled with broke college students and retirees. I'll have you all replaced before you've walked out the door."

She doesn't have a comeback ready.

I know I'm being an asshole. My uncle left the company's finances straggling above the red, way too close for comfort. Instead of prioritizing profit margins, he put his focus on the fun. He loved all the employee appreciation and extravagance.

It's not like I wanted to take away the staff holiday party. In fact, I honestly don't care one way or another. But we don't have the funds for much more than the typical shitty corporate pizza party.

I'd rather not.

While I'm busy musing internally, Noel looks as if she's contemplating stomping out of my office.

Part of me wants her to. Save me the frustration of seeing this cute little elf look at me with hatred every single day. The other part of me–the part that lies south of my stomach–would hate not getting to take in her rage regularly.

"Now, if you'll excuse me, I have work to do," I say dismissively.

She rolls her eyes and heads for the door of my office only to stop and turn back at the doorway. She looks at me with pure disdain.

"Yeah, keep pretending you have *work* to do. I'd hate for anyone to find out that Santa is really just a dirty little slut."

three

Kane

This is my second season working at SantaScape and it's shaping up to be even better than the last.

There aren't many employees at SantaScape that work year-round. Most of us are seasonal and use it as a chance to earn some extra cash for the holidays. I work as a content developer for startup companies and the last quarter is usually pretty slow.

So last year, Eve put in a good word for me with her boss and I spent six weeks of the holiday season helping out wherever they needed. Sometimes I work as security because for some reason, the happiest time of the year is also when some people turn into the biggest assholes. Other times I fill in as Santa or even a snow monster.

No matter what, I find a way to enjoy what I do.

Eve worked full-time for Mr. Bates for two years before he retired. Now, he's enjoying life outside these walls which he's earned.

However, the transition of his nephew hasn't been easy on everyone.

For me, it's been fine. I come to work and do whatever job I'm supposed to for the day.

It helps that most of the time, I share the same schedule as Eve. Getting to share a ride home with my partner at the end of a shift is pretty awesome. Among the other things we share.

For instance, the elf I'm currently waiting for in the shadows like a weirdo.

Meeting Noel last year was awesome. She was up for a good time and we had no problem showing her one.

She typically works as a bartender or server because says a career is more terrifying to commit to than a relationship.

Since last holiday season, we've seen her a number of times. The occasional dinner and hookup. She's even included Eve in her girl's nights with her best friend. But nothing too serious.

Eve and I pride ourselves on how smooth and fluid our relationship works. Most of the time, we prefer to invite new people in our bed together by finding someone at the private club we hold a membership for.

We got really lucky when we met Noel. It's not often we find someone outside of the club, in fact, it's only happened twice. Her and Nico.

Over the years we've found playmates that go into our trusted list. Those very few individuals are safe people that neither of us has ever felt would dishonor our relationship.

If our love for each other eventually grows into something more with another or two, we're willing to figure it out. But I know that I'll always have her and she will always have me.

Recently, our boss joined that list.

MOST OF THE office still calls him Nicholas but I guess sucking his dick and letting him fuck my ass earned me the privilege to use his nickname.

HE'S NOT SO bad but I can empathize with how challenging taking over a new company must be.

NOT EVERYONE IS willing to cut him a break.

FROM MY SPOT in the hallway, I can hear Noel's parting quip before she slams his door closed.

"SLUT SHAMING SEEMS BENEATH YOU, NOEL," I say as I catch her stomping her way through the hallway.

She startles before seeing it's me and then she snorts. "Since when?"

I expect her attitude. Noel isn't exactly known for being chill and reasonable around here. She's energetic and fun and sweet as candy when she's in character. But I've seen her put someone in their place for trying to cut the line or scolding someone for unwanted advances on an employee.

"Since we both know just how much you like to be called a dirty little slut while being double-teamed." I wiggle my brows at her.

Noel scoffs. "Yeah, well, that's different."

"Is it different because you hate Nico? Or because you're pretending like you can't stand him when you really want to hate-fuck him?" I ask with a cocky tone.

I'm not an idiot. I can see their attraction to one another.

When Mr. Bates held our annual staff meeting last month and announced that his nephew would be taking over for him, I was sitting in the back with her talking about how hot he was.

Then he opened his mouth and the first thing he did was announce a change in our uniform design.

The new material is cheaper judging by how uncomfortable it is, so that didn't do him any favors. Especially those of us who have worn the higher quality costumes. If I had to guess, it was probably a cost cutting measure.

Just like all of his changes since.

"I do not want to hate-fuck him," she denies.

She's adorable when she's trying to throw a tantrum.

Rolling my eyes, I say, "Okay, just regular fuck him then."

I know I'm right. She knows I'm right.

Yet only one of us isn't living in delusion.

And it's not the one with killer tits and a tight ass.

"Whatever. I should tell the whole office that Nicholas is canceling our Christmas party so he can spend that extra time fucking his secretary and her boyfriend."

I don't miss the way she says his name like she might vomit but I'm more focused on the end of her statement.

Grabbing Noel by the shoulders, I stop her and look at her face-to-face.

"First, you know that Eve and I prefer the term partners due to our lifestyle choices," I say with a raised brow, pleased when she looks chastised. "Second, you would never tell anyone something like that because he's not doing anything different than what you've done before yourself."

Noel isn't deterred by me throwing our history into the conversation. "I'm not the one trying to ruin this Christmas season, though, am I?"

"Noel, it's just a fucking party. We can all go get drunk at the bar across the street that night instead. I'll even buy your drinks all night long as if it's an open bar. And then after, maybe we can have a repeat of that thing we did after last year's party."

I'm trying my best to boost the mood and my offer is genuine.

Her interest does seem to peak, but then her shoulders drop. "It's not the fucking same, Kane."

I know it's not. While Noel usually only acts serious when she absolutely has to, I can see that all the changes Nico is making are getting under her skin.

She loves this place so I understand not wanting it to be any different than what she's used to but honestly, it seems like she's taking everything personally.

Trying again to dissipate some of her frustration, I pull her in for a hug. "Listen, I know it's not exactly what you're used to. We can still make the most of it. Without you spilling the details on our boss's sex life."

She steps out of my hold and crosses her arms over her chest, "Why not?"

I can't help but look down at the way her movement lifts her perfect tits before moving my eyes back up to her face and I can tell she's no longer serious about the idea. "Because even if it could be chalked up to office gossip, it's never a good idea to spread sex rumors. Unless they're about us."

I say that last line with a wink and watch as her shoulders deflate with defeat.

She sighs, "You know. I probably wouldn't have said anything anyway."

"I know you wouldn't have, Noel." I might be acting like I'm talking her off the ledge here but I don't believe she'd ever publicly humiliate someone for their sexual exploits.

She would never want to hurt Eve. I don't think she wants to hurt me either but it's rarely the men who get the worst of the backlash.

Noel spent one of our date nights telling us all about her best friend who openly has multiple boyfriends. They've faced some serious prejudice over what I consider to be a beautiful relationship between all consenting adults.

"Besides," I add, "you know you'd rather join us."

She looks at me as if I've said something insane. "Absolutely not."

"Why not?" I ask. The sexual tension between the two of them will eventually explode and I have a feeling it'll happen sooner than later.

"Because it's not the same as hooking up with you and Eve. I don't...dislike the two of you." She says with a roguish smile.

"That's because you got to know us. Maybe you should try getting to know the boss, too," I tease her. I have a feeling if she spends some time with Nico, she won't hate him as much as she's pretending she does.

And maybe, that could lead to fun for all of us.

four

"*N*ico, I need to step away for a few minutes," I announce as I pop my head into his office.

He never minds when I take a break but I still give him the courtesy of letting him know. While I do let the man fuck me occasionally, I'm also really good at my job.

Working for Mr. Bates was a little different. For instance, he was happily–and monogamously–married with no desire to lure me into his office with the promise of multiple orgasms or threesomes.

It didn't take long for Nico to figure out my interests.

What can I say? I'm a team player and love group activities.

Usually, Kane and I attend the one club in town that caters to those particular needs but I also like to indulge here in the office.

It helps that my long-term partner in crime, Kane, also happens to work in the same building. I got him the job last

Drea Denae

year and it didn't take more than a week before he introduced me to Noel.

We've had plenty of fun but she's not one to make long-term commitments, sticking to the occasional date or hookup.

I've met her best friend and attended some of their very platonic girls' nights but other than that, it's been very casual.

Noel just hasn't ever seemed interested in more than sex and friendship. Not that I'm judging.

Kane and I have a very unique relationship. One where we not only like to fuck each other but also add in the occasional extra dick or pussy.

Which reminds me of the task at hand.

The elevator ride doesn't take long before the doors open to the lobby and the sounds of families waiting to meet Santa and his elves fill the space. Some are excited, some are nervous. Some are screaming out in frustration and fear.

I'm so happy to work several floors away from all this noise.

I use my badge to scan through a side entrance, where the employee dressing rooms are located.

Most employees will already be at their stations, waiting to greet each of Santa's guests. However, I know that the one I happen to be looking for will be rushing to her spot with milliseconds to spare.

It helps to know someone's habits when you're searching them out for nefarious behavior. And luckily, she's exactly where I thought she'd be.

I take the time to watch her while I'm still unnoticed.

At the mirror, she's rushing through her makeup routine. She doesn't add much, just enough to fit the part. Though, there's not much that could dress up those terrible new costumes.

I watch as she struggles to straighten up her ears and hat.

It makes me think about how last year she used those same pointy ears to cosplay for a particular fantasy I had. Her stockings are green and white striped, running up her legs that I've spent plenty of time between.

"Are you going to stand there and stare or did you come down here for something in particular?" she teases.

I won't deny that I've been worried about her reaction since she walked into Nico's office earlier today. While Kane and I have plenty of partners we play with, occasionally we find one to keep around long-term or offer a repeat rendezvous. We never make them promises and they appear content with that agreement.

And despite how casual Noel wants to keep things, she's special to us both.

She's feisty enough in and out of the bedroom that we never get bored with her. And she's happy to indulge in whatever scenario we've come up with. That's why she's one of the few partners we're both allowed to play with solo.

"I wanted to check on you. You were very upset earlier," I tell her honestly.

Noel stops messing with her costume and turns to look at me. "I was upset with that asshole, not what I walked in on."

Nodding, I approach her slowly like she's a frightened animal. "How are you feeling now that you've had some time to calm down?"

My words are a genuine question but I try to add a flirtatious inflection to my tone. Luckily, Kane filled me in on their conversation so I know she's not truly upset with me. I want to make sure she understands that just because she caught us with Nico, we're not attempting to end our ongoing activities with her.

She's quick to catch on and the sparkle in her eyes tells me she's happy to play my game. "I guess I was a little bit...disappointed."

"How did we disappoint you?" I fake a pout as I step as close as I can without actually touching her.

"For starters, you know how much I like to share that sweet little pussy with Kane." Her tone is chiding as she sneaks a hand under my skirt. Her finger pushes my panties to the side. "You're still soaking wet, too. Is this for them or me?"

"All of you," I admit as I lick my lips, feeling desperate despite being completely satisfied when I walked in here. "All three of you make me so fucking wet."

Her fingers move my panties back in place before she taps me over them, like a gentle spank. "Well, I think you've been given enough for today. Though I am tempted to get down on my knees and show you how much better I can do than either of them."

She might sound cocky but she isn't wrong. No one has ever made me come harder with their mouth than Noel.

I whimper as she removes her hand from my skirt, only to place it on my neck.

"What do you want, Eve? Did you come down here just so I can see how swollen your lips still look even hours after you let that big cock fuck your mouth?"

There's a thread of anger in her voice but I don't know if she's jealous that I was hooking up with someone else or because she wishes she had been the one taking Nico's cock. Time to test my theories.

"I can still taste him, you know? I know you like to share, Noel. Want to see if you can taste him too?"

Her hand tightens on my neck and I moan, not caring if I get loud. Anyone could walk in but they shouldn't. And if they did, I would drip onto the floor. I fucking love to be watched.

Those thoughts are melted from my brain when she drags my mouth to hers. Her tongue dips into my mouth, searching for the taste that I teased her with. Her hand skirts from my throat to the back of my neck to grip my hair.

Even though we're standing face to face, I want her closer. My hands land on her hips, pulling her body into mine so that every inch of us possible is touching.

She pulls away from our kiss, grabbing my bottom lip with her teeth before letting it go. The action leaves a sting, weaving in a little pain with our pleasure.

"You're going to get on your knees and eat my cunt like a good girl, Eve. Then you're going to take your cute little ass back upstairs and kiss your boss."

Before I drop down, she grabs her jacket off the nearby bench, putting it on the ground to protect my knees. Once I'm situated, one of her legs wraps around my shoulder, getting her wide open for me.

Her panties are thin and I'm tempted to rip them off of her. But she's got a part to play once I'm done here and she really shouldn't be everyone's favorite elf around all those little ones without any panties. So I move them over like she just did for me just moments ago.

My tongue darts out, circling her clit first before flattening and licking her slit from top to bottom.

Noel moans and grabs my hair, pulling my face even closer as if to direct me on how to please her.

But I know what she likes.

She's soaking already and I use two fingers to gather some of that wetness before moving them behind her to circle her rim.

"Fuck. Such a good slut for me, Eve. Trying to fuck my ass with your fingers while you lick my pussy like you're starving."

Her words do exactly what she knows they will, encouraging me to keep going.

My tongue darts in and out of her hole while my fingers do the same to her back entrance.

Noel loves ass play. I've fucked her there with my fingers, mouth, and plenty of toys. I've watched Kane fuck her there while I licked her clit. I've used a strap-on to fuck her ass while Kane fucked her pussy. She loses her mind every time.

Fuck, even thinking about it has me wanting to touch myself.

"Don't you dare. That greedy little cunt has had enough today." As if reading my thoughts, she forbids me to act on my own pleasure.

Which makes me wetter.

I suck on her clit while I debate begging her to let me grind myself on her leg.

Deciding against it, I put all my focus into making her come. I know she's close when she tugs on my hair and starts riding against my face.

"That's it. Right *there*. Oh such a good girl, Eve."

I lick everything she gives me until she's panting her way through the aftershocks.

I kiss her gently before moving her panties back into place. Then I climb out from her skirt and stand up, licking my lips as she watches.

"Is that better?" I ask playfully, raising one brow.

"You're lucky I have to get out there or I'd throw you to the ground and ride your face until you can't breathe," she says as she turns back to the mirror and makes sure everything is where it should be.

"Promises, promises," I taunt back.

"I have to go but yes, we're good," she twists to face me again before wrinkling her face up in irritation. "I just...can't stand him, Eve."

"He's not as bad as you think. And I don't just mean because he fucks like a god. Maybe you should try to get to know him before judging him over a few changes."

She looks at me like she's thinking it over before smiling sarcastically. "No thanks."

I roll my eyes at her.

"Anyways, I have to go. But don't forget to give the boss a kiss for me," she says as she cackles her way out of the dressing room.

I *am* a good girl. I better follow those orders.

five

J watch the security camera to see Noel bounce out of the dressing room just one minute before the doors are supposed to open to SantaScape.

Then I see Eve leave right after, her hair and makeup slightly awry.

I don't know what they were doing but whatever it was, I'm certain it wouldn't get either of them on the nice list.

Part of me is aggravated that my secretary most likely stepped away from her desk to fool around with another employee. That might make me a little hypocritical but I don't care. I'm more annoyed that I didn't get to watch or participate in any of it.

Noel has been a pain in my ass since the day I stepped into this office. I can understand that not everyone likes change but as grown adults, I would like to think we're adaptable.

Then again, my employees play dress up for a living.

Concentrating on my screen again, I watch Noel greet guest after guest, giving them genuine smiles.

I'm man enough to admit that I hate watching her give something to these strangers that she's never given me. I'm also man enough to admit that I'm hoping that will change.

I wait until I hear Eve's chair moving along the hardwood floors, signaling her return to her desk, before calling for her to join me in my office.

"Eve," I say with authority. It might be her name but we both know it's also a demand.

She doesn't disappoint me as she complies, walking into my office with her hips swaying. As if her desk was merely a pit stop and I was her destination all along.

"I sure hope whatever matter that you needed to attend to was important," I say with a bit of bite in my tone.

Eve circles my desk and I push my chair out, making the space for her to step between my legs.

Without saying a word, she leans down and kisses me.

I understand her intention immediately once the sweetness of what I assume is Noel's orgasm hits my lips. Groaning against her mouth, I'm desperate for every bit of the taste.

My hands fist in her hair, fusing us together. We only break apart once I'm convinced there's no remnants of Noel left for me to devour.

"Thank you," I tell her genuinely.

She winks at me. "You're welcome. But you should know I was just following orders."

"Fuck." My head leans back against my chair. "That little-"

"That little what?" Eve asks with a hint of warning while taking a seat in my lap.

"I was going to say brat." I'm pretty sure I was, anyway.

She laughs as she leans against me. "Glad I could be your conduit, getting you a taste of what you really wanted."

I know she doesn't mean anything by it but it still rubs me the wrong way. It sounds like she's a consolation prize.

Just because I'm attracted to Noel doesn't make me any less interested in her or Kane.

"Hey," I say, lifting her chin until she meets my eyes. "I want you just as bad as I want her. Just as bad as I want Kane. No one is a substitute for my desires in this situation."

We don't label this thing. Her and Kane have their rules and I follow them. I'm just not going to let either of them think I'm using them to fill a space until I figure out a way to get someone else underneath me.

"I didn't mean that, Nico. I was joking," she says with a reassuring smile and I believe her.

I might not have any idea what the future of SantaScape looks like but I do hope that even after I leave, I'll still get to spend time with Kane and Eve.

And maybe a naughty little elf.

COMING HOME to a quiet house used to be comforting but now it feels... pathetic.

I used to enjoy the solace that a peaceful place offered. I walk through the door, put my things away and either order delivery or cook. Then I find some sort of work that could have waited until tomorrow but I do it anyway.

Occasionally, I go out and find someone to spend my night with only to leave them in the morning.

Now, I crave...more.

I worked for a major corporation as a business analyst up until a few months ago. I actually enjoyed it too.

Sadly, they needed to make cuts and I was deemed unnecessary.

Ironically, I was the one who handed them a list of cost-cutting measures. Typically, layoffs are a last resort but they decided to escalate matters immediately.

Only after I left did I start to realize how drained I felt. Work was my life.

I graduated with my degree and went into the workforce head first, never really stopping to think about my life outside the office.

On my first day of unemployment, I woke up and realized how empty my world felt.

Then my uncle called. He told me Jack had an emergency and he needed someone he could count on to cover for him.

He suggested that we not tell the employees my role was only temporary. He didn't believe that the employees would be willing to follow someone they knew had one foot out the door.

I'm not sure I believe it's pure coincidence. He could have found any number of people to interview for the role but instead, he handed it to his nephew who specializes in the very thing he desperately needed.

Except he couldn't have known that I'm completely burned out and haven't been able to think of anything outside the obvious steps to take.

I've done everything I can but the fact of the matter is, a seasonal business isn't going to generate enough revenue to last forever.

We cater to one holiday for a six to eight-week period of the year.

The full-time staff we do have is minimal and essential to the operation.

I have a few weeks to find a way to save my family's company. The pressure is high. My uncle built this company himself.

Every member of his staff has always loved him. I've never heard him say a bad word about any of them either. His desire to take care of them shows just how tight of a community he built and I'll be the one to ruin it all.

I can't even bring myself to fix something to eat tonight. Instead, I strip down and head for the bathroom, ready to wash the day off me. If only I could wash off all of the expectations that everyone has for me, including myself.

Once I step into the warm water, I let myself think of Noel, Kane and Eve. Even the banter with Noel has a little bit of the joy I used to feel at work seeping through.

I let my mind wander as I stand under the water, thinking about how I wish that she would have done more than stand in the doorway when she interrupted us.

The thought has me grabbing my dick. I'm already hard, ready to go as if I can somehow will my desire to reality.

Would she walk in so Eve could share my length with her, allowing them both to use their mouths on me? Would she have taken over for Kane, using her mouth on Eve while bending over and letting Kane fuck her from behind? Would she pull me away and beg me to make her come, however I want?

I remember the way she tasted on Eve's lips and I imagine what it would have been like to see Eve on her knees for Noel. Was she controlling or gentle? Did she cry out with pleasure? Or would she have tried to hold back out of the fear of getting caught?

It takes me no time at all before my release flows over my hand as I groan.

"*Fuck.*"

As I finish my shower, I make a decision.

Maybe I'm not going to save the business–though I won't stop trying–but that won't be the only thing I'm fighting for this holiday season.

I'm ready to chase after that elf.

six

"So he practically ate your face?" I ask Eve as I kiss my way down her body.

She lets out a gasp as my flattened tongue runs over her nipple before I pull it between my teeth. "Devoured me. Like the flavor of her pussy on my tongue was his last meal."

When Eve told me she had a visit with Noel after we were caught earlier today, I stripped off her clothes. This woman is my closest friend, my favorite person to fuck and one of the sexiest people I've ever met.

We've done this before, talked about a recent sexual encounter as foreplay. Or even recreated something. We've done those things many times.

It's one of the hottest things we do because it feels like even when we aren't doing something together, we're somehow involving the other person. It's a special level of trust to share a partner and to know we can tell each other anything? That's fucking awesome.

41

"Tell me what she said to you again?" I ask while moving my attention to her other breast. I haven't forgotten anything, I just want to hear her say the words again in her needy voice.

"She told me to eat her cunt and then go kiss him." Eve's hands grab the back of my head, encouraging me to suck harder and for a few moments, I do.

Then I lift myself up to hover over her on the bed, "Did you do a good job?" I ask with a playful smirk.

Eve scoffs, telling me I should know better.

And I do. We both know she's an expert at oral. I might not have a pussy to speak from personal experience, but I've watched her bring plenty of partners to orgasm with her mouth. Besides, she's just as talented with a cock.

"She came so hard, she flooded my tongue," she says as she adjusts to fit my cock at her entrance.

I thrust into her and we both let out sounds of satisfaction. No matter how many times we do this, no matter how many other people we play with, sliding into her feels fucking incredible every time.

"I wish I could have watched." I do. I could have sat in the corner and jacked off. I didn't even need to touch anyone but myself. Just seeing them would have been enough for me.

Eve moans, "Me too."

"Noel didn't let you come, though, did she?" I ask, taunting her.

Her cunt tightens around me, trying to chase the release it was denied earlier.

"No. I wanted to so bad, babe." Her tongue runs up my neck before her mouth lands right by my ear as she tells me, "I wanted to grind myself on her leg, I felt so desperate for it."

Her arms wrap around my back, attempting to pull me closer.

I'm torn between fucking her hard and fast or trying to slow this down to make it last. I guess I can try todo a little of everything.

"I'll give you what you need now, baby girl. I'm going to fuck you so good that you'll soak the sheets."

Eve's eyes light up with joy before I pull out and flip her over.

Leaning over to the bedside table, I grab a bottle of lubricant and her favorite clitoral stimulator from the drawer.

I line my cock back up with her entrance while dripping some of the product onto her puckered hole. Tossing the bottle aside, I fuck her leisurely as I use two fingers to prep her ass.

My girl loves to be fucked in the ass while I suction a toy over her clit.We do this often enough that it doesn't take long before she's ready.

Eve moans in anticipation as I pull out again.

"You ready for me to fuck your tight little asshole, baby girl?" I ask her.

Her head nods but I want her to beg.

"You want me to fuck your ass?" I ask again as I slap her ass cheek,

"Please, please, please." She's desperate and begging, just how I want her. "Fuck my ass, Kane."

I'm careful as I work myself inside, not wanting to hurt her. Once I've pushed past the tight ring, I start with shallow thrusts.

"Poor thing. Only one orgasm today and you're begging like a slut for more." She loves her anal sex with a side of degradation.

Nico is much more natural at that particular skill than I am but I've been fucking her for much longer. I know what words do it for her.

Grabbing the toy from earlier, I lean down and maneuver my arm around her waist while increasing my pace. The toy suctions onto her and she lets out another loud moan as chills break out over her skin.

"That's right baby, take this dick in your ass like a filthy little whore." I bite out the words, trying to hold back my own orgasm.

I slap her ass again with the hand that isn't holding the toy before using it to grab ahold of her hair. I use my grip to pull her up until her back is against my chest.

"Please, Kane. I'm so close," she whines.

"I know, baby. I'm going to give you what you want." I say against her ear before turning up the power on the toy.

Our angle is a little awkward but we've perfected this position over time. I can look over her shoulder while keeping the grip on her hair. She loves the bite of pain and I'm counting on it to bring her over the edge.

"That's it, Eve. Come for me, baby girl. Fucking soak me."

The words do the trick and I feel the gush of liquid down both of our thighs.

A gift for you

Enjoy your gift! From Mother

amazon Gift Receipt

Scan the QR code to learn more about your gift or start a return.

Santa Is A Sl*t (Holiday Hoemies)
Order ID: 111-4083746-5591423   Ordered on November 22, 2024

I toss the toy to the side before pushing her back down on the bed and grabbing onto her hips. It doesn't take me more than a few more thrusts before I'm coming inside her ass.

Before we both pass out, I find myself wondering if I could convince Nico to eat my cum out of her ass tomorrow morning.

seven

NOEL

T open a bottle of wine while I wait for my phone to ring.

After I left work today, I sent a text to Val asking if we could video chat tonight and she responded with ten thumbs-up emojis.

Maybe she feels guilty for abandoning me. Or maybe she's just the best friend a girl can have and she would have called me anyway.

But I want to be petty for at least one whole day before I start to move on to the acceptance stage.

My phone starts to sing about big booty bitches just as I am taking a seat on the couch and I swipe to answer it.

Her face lights up my phone screen as I make myself comfort-able, squirming around until it feels just right.

"What happened today that made you send me all those crude emoji scenes?" Her words are enthusiastic and demanding, wanting to know all the dirty details.

I might have sent her a text with two eggplants, a kitty cat crying, a tongue and a ton of water droplets with no other information except what time I'd be free to explain it to her.

"Oh hey, Val. How are you? How was your day?" I ask casually, pretending to observe the societal standard of pleasantries before diving into the gossip.

"Yeah, yeah, whatever. Spill it." She's sitting in her living room with her own glass of wine.

It's only a matter of time before one or more of her boyfriends join her and I want her full attention until then.

Adding my signature flare and using my superior storytelling capabilities, I outline every single detail of walking in on the scene in Nicholas's office. I even grab a pen and paper to show her a stick figure recreation.

I do not doubt that if Val hasn't already been in that position before, she will be testing it out as early as tomorrow.

I can hardly believe it myself but watching Val's reactions to the story makes me giggle. The total shock and surprise on her facial features are hilarious, especially when she spits wine out on her blouse when I get to the part about Eve's locker room visit.

"Well, what are you going to do?" She asks once I've finished talking.

"There's not much I can do. It's not like I want to embarrass Kane and Eve and there's no way for me to use it against Nicholas without hurting them," I shrug nonchalantly. "Besides, it's probably not the best idea to spread rumors about anyone's sex life but especially my boss."

Val raises her brow at me skeptically. "Really?"

Nodding, I ask, "What?"

"Nothing...it's just that I'm surprised at how mature you're being."

"What's that supposed to mean?" I take a little offense at her statement.

"It's not that you're immature, Noel. It's that you tend to thrive in chaos and most of the time maturity doesn't overlap with your brand of chaos." She tells me with a sympathetic purse of her lips.

I know what she means, even if it stings a little. There's a reason Val's guys like to grill me before our girl's nights. I've gotten into plenty of trouble over the years and Val didn't have a choice but to join me. Either she was right beside me or figuring a way to get me out of whatever compromising position I found myself in.

"I guess I've grown," I say cockily.

But the truth is, I think I am growing. Even if I've never imagined settling down like Val has, I know I'm going to have to take life a little more seriously sooner or later.

It had already crossed my mind that this might be my last season at SantaScape. Eventually, I am going to need to do more than temporary positions in order to have a reliable income.

This place is going to be a lot harder to afford once I'm paying rent on my own.

"We both have, Noel. It was only a matter of time before adulthood caught up to us." My best friend tells me proudly.

Val has always been the more sensible one between the two of us but she never made me feel bad about who I am.

"Maybe so," I say, steering away from the seriousness of the conversation, "But I've learned something really important today."

"What's that?"

My smile is wider than the Joker's. "That our new Santa is a dirty little slut."

We both fall into giggles until tears start to form in my eyes.

Once we've calmed down, Val asks me, "So when do you think you'll fuck your boss? I have to say, I highly recommend it. In fact, I think you're the one who encouraged me to fuck all three of my bosses."

Of course, she uses my good intentions against me. I just wanted my friend to get laid.

"Why does everyone think I want to fuck him?" I try to infuse confusion into my tone.

"You're totally going to fuck him. I bet you have a foursome by the end of the week," she says with a smug smile.

If I last that long, I'll be impressed. I'm not sure that the next time one of the three of them attempts to seduce me, I'd be able to deny them.

I'm not in the habit of turning down an orgasm.

We eventually change the subject, talking about the rest of our day before making plans to have another video chat later this week.

I put away my wine glass before changing into a pair of pajamas with candy canes all over them. My love for the holiday season goes deep. I can't remember a time when I didn't love everything about it.

Laying down in bed, the thought crosses my mind that this will be my first Christmas that I wake up all alone. When I turn off the light and close my eyes, I try to pretend that the apartment isn't as empty as it feels.

* * *

THE NEXT MORNING, I decide to start fresh. Walking into work, I start to think about how there's no reason for me to hold on to things I can't change.

I can't change the fact that my roommate is in a happy relationship and wants to take it to the next level. I can't change the fact that my boss is an asshole who seems to be determined to ruin everything about the job I love. I definitely can't change the fact that the memory of Eve sucking Nicholas's dick while Kane ate her pussy is seared into my brain. And I really can't change the fact I want a chance to join them.

That's right. I've finally accepted that I do want to fuck my boss.

And Eve.

And Kane.

Because even if it doesn't last past the holidays, I don't want to spend the next few weeks alone. I want to spend it getting naked with attractive people and collecting orgasms like book nerds collect special edition books.

I just have to figure out a way to make it happen.

I'm still working on my course of action when I bump into someone. And as luck would have it, I look up into the eyes of my boss.

Why do I want to giggle like a schoolgirl who just saw her crush changing in the locker room?

Oh, probably because I saw his dick yesterday and now I have to try and keep a straight face while having a conversation with him right after I was thinking about how hard I want him to rail me.

Clearing my throat, I say, "Excuse me."

"Would you mind if I spoke with you for a minute?" Nicholas's voice is monotone, making it difficult to determine if he's still angry with me.

I'm not sure if this is the best timing to have a private conversation with him but I guess it's necessary considering the circumstances.

"Sure," I say with uncertainty.

"Great. Let's head to my office." Still, his tone gives nothing away.

I look at him skeptically and whisper yell, "You want to go to the scene of the crime?"

Nicholas rolls his eyes. "Hilarious, Noel."

I sure as fuck thought so, I think to myself as we enter the elevator. He pushes the button for his floor and I try to discreetly study him from the corner of my eye.

He's handsome. I can understand my attraction to him. There's an energy around him that gives off dominance, which was confirmed after hearing him threaten to edge Kane and Eve yesterday.

Then again, he was just fucking Eve's face, which requires very little effort on his end. So he could be a lazy lay.

I doubt it, though.

The elevator dings, letting us know we've reached our destination floor and I follow him to his office. Eve is at her desk and she blows me a kiss when we pass her. I pretend to catch it and then pat the area just below my navel while I wink at her.

It makes me think of how she was kissing me there yesterday afternoon and I'm curious to know if she followed my orders.

Nicholas waves me ahead of him before stepping into the room himself and closing the door behind us. "Take a seat."

I want to make a comment about saying please but I know it's just going to irritate him and I still don't know exactly what this conversation is about.

"Now, where should we start, Noel?" He asks with a tsk. "Barging into a private office? Insubordination? Unprofessional conduct?"

My eyes go wide in shock at his audacity before I let out a loud snort. "Is this a joke?"

It has to be. Unprofessional conduct? I literally caught this man with his pants down yesterday.

"I assure you that I do not find your unprofessional behavior a joking manner whatsoever." His voice is stern.

I expected some backlash for yesterday's events but this feels much more serious than I thought it would be.

"I'm sorry?" I say it as a question because I am truly confused by this situation.

"What exactly is it that you're sorry for?" He asks while leaning back in his chair.

There's this instinct deep inside of me that wants to do the right thing here and potentially save my job. But then there's the devil on my shoulder telling me to apologize for nothing.

He saves me from having to choose between the two by speaking as if his question was always rhetorical.

"Are you sorry that you walked in on me having play time with Kane and Eve? Or that you weren't Included?"

Umm...what?

"Or are you maybe sorry that you came all over Eve's lips and didn't leave enough of a taste to satisfy my craving?"

Suddenly, this feels much more dangerous than the idea of losing my job.

It feels like my boss might be trying, and succeeding, to turn me on.

Standing from his chair, he rounds his desk until he's right in front of me. "Are you sorry for any of those things, my naughty little elf?"

His naughty little elf?

I lick my lips and decide to lean into whatever game he's trying to play. "No. I'm not sorry."

The smirk on his face tells me he was expecting my answer. "Then maybe I should do something to make you sorry."

Now I'm back to being confused. "Are you going to fire me?"

He chuckles. "No, I'm not going to fire you. That would probably be the smart thing to do. A reasonable punishment for your actions. But I've got another idea."

"Then what is it?"

"I'm still going to punish you. I think ten will do." He says as he shrugs off his suit jacket and begins to roll up his sleeves.

"Ten swats over your ass."

I might have just had a spontaneous orgasm. As a proud brat, I fucking love to be spanked. Quickly, I pinch myself because there's no way that this isn't a dream.

My boss, who is a very sexy asshole, wants to spank me as a punishment for...turning him on.

"Alright, big man, I'll let you dole out your punishment on one condition."

He gestures for me to continue.

"Admit that you want me first. Tell me that when you saw me walk into this room yesterday that you would have given anything to see me drop to my knees and share your cock with Eve like a lollipop. Tell me how hard it made you when she kissed you with my taste still on her lips."

I need this. Before I give this man the power to put me in a vulnerable position, I need him to give me some of the control in this scenario.

He gently places his hand on my cheek and looks me in the eyes as he says, "I don't want you, Noel. I fucking need you."

Smiling at my small victory, I back away from him and watch as a flicker of disappointment flashes over his features.

Then I watch the heat light back up in his eyes as I bend over his desk. "Then spank me, Santa." I wink to let him know that

He chuckles, laughing at my cheeky comment, helping to lighten the moment.

I'm happy I didn't have time to change into my costume yet, I don't think this would be quite as sexy with candy cane striped tights on. Or maybe it would. Instead, I have on a loose sweater dress which manages to give him easy access when he lifts the hem and studies my ass.

"Make sure you count out loud for me, I'd hate to lose track and start all over." His tone tells me the opposite, I'm sure he'd be delighted if I gave him a reason to repeat this.

His hand gently caresses one of my ass cheeks before giving it a soft squeeze. Then, a slap comes down hard, making me jump a little. "Count."

"One."

He repeats the process and I continue to count.

When the word, "ten," leaves my mouth, he begins to massage the pain away.

I'm uncomfortable, but not because what we did hurt me. Instead, I need relief.

"What do you need, Noel?" His words demand an answer.

"Please make me come." I'm not going to be shy about what I need here. I never have been and I won't be starting today.

"Good girl. Now do I use my fingers or my mouth?"

I want to beg him to use both but before I can, two fingers are sliding inside my entrance. I'm already drenched, so turned on from the spanking he gave me, that he enters me with ease.

"Soaking wet, just like I thought you would be. Does my naughty elf like to be punished?"

There he goes with the possessiveness again.

"Yes," I say but it comes out as more of a moan.

I think about how Eve is just outside this door, probably listening in on what we're doing. Or maybe even peeking through a crack in the door.

"Look at you, squeezing my fingers like a needy little slut. Come on them."

He curls his fingers in just the right spot and I'm seeing spots in my vision, following his order. "Fuck, Nicholas." This encounter has been so hot, I can only imagine the mess I've made.

Turning around, I watch as he sucks every bit of my off his fingers, leaving nothing behind.

"Even better when it comes straight from the source." I don't know if his pun was intentional, but I smile back at him.

Then I notice the clock on the wall and realize I'm about to be late for my shift and I still need to change into my costume.

"Fuck, I have to go," I tell him as I fix my clothing.

"Alright, but we do need to have a real conversation at some point. And Noel?"

I stop and turn to face him.

"Since I know what you taste like, I think it's best if you call me, Nico." The cocky look on his face makes me wish I had more time to put his mouth to better use.

Instead, I roll my eyes before rushing out of the room. I can only hope all of our conversations end with the same present.

eight

*W*atching Noel rush out of Nico's office this morning has me feeling giddy. His office does a decent job of hiding the noise but I heard just enough to understand what they were getting up to in there.

Step one is complete. Those two just needed to be in a confined space long enough to give in to their sexual tension. It's about damn time.

Now, I just need all of us to figure out a way to have some fun together. And lucky for me, I have the perfect partner in crime to assist me.

Nico has already warned me he'd be working late tonight and both Kane and Noel are about to finish up their closing shifts downstairs.

Soon, it will be Nico down there, playing the part of Santa. His uncle established the tradition years ago and I've convinced him he has to carry it on. Especially since he's already changed so much here.

59

I know him just enough to know that he has to have a reason but he hasn't given me any additional information. My instincts tell me to trust him and they are rarely wrong.

I send Kane a text, asking him if he's ready. I get a thumbs up in response.

Nico's just heading out of his office when I look up. Perfect timing.

"Sorry to do this to you, Nico, but one of the security guards just called up and said that there was a matter down there that needed your attention."

There's a chance he knows I'm lying but he decides to go along with it anyway. "Whatever it is, I hope it doesn't take too long."

"I'll go with you. If it's something I can handle, you'll be able to head home. I was waiting for Kane to shower anyway."

No, I wasn't but I'm fully invested in our plans which means I need to continue this charade.

Nico gives me a curious look on the elevator ride down but doesn't say anything.

I'm glad he doesn't press me for details because I'm too excited that I'd probably ruin the whole surprise.

"Where is security meeting us?" He asks as he follows me through the different holiday scene setups.

"Over near the sleigh," I tell him, trying to keep my voice as normal as possible.

As we round the last corner, Kane and Noel come into view. The sight is so much better than I ever could have imagined.

Noel sits on the bench inside Santa's sleigh with a bow around her neck resembling a collar. She's completely naked and Kane has managed some impressive impromptu restraints. Her legs are held open, leaving her on full display.

My partner in crime is at the head of the sleigh, also completely naked. He's bent over the front railing, giving him a perfect view of Noel. A bottle of lube sits on the ground near his feet because of course, he thought of everything. And my personal favorite piece of decor, tying all of this together like the best present ever, is the shiny butt plug on display from his position.

"Surprise!" I announce while jumping up and down in glee.

Nico's eyes are wide as he takes in the scene.

"Don't worry, I already called the cleaning crew and told them we would be delaying their services by two hours tonight," I say with pride. I might have a lot of fun at work but that's only because I'm a bad bitch when it comes to getting things done.

"What is this?" Nico's voice is laced with confusion but I can hear an undertone of excitement.

"I thought we could use some motivation to really get into the holiday spirit," I say as I make my way over to Kane. "Good job, babe."

He winks at me, "Anything for you."

I lean over to kiss him before pulling away and turning back to Nico while reaching into my bra for the condom I took out of his drawer earlier today. Handing it over to him, I proudly tell him, "As you can see, I prepped him for you."

Turning back, I wave my hand around Kane's ass like it's a grand prize on a game show.

"I see that," he says. He closes the space between us and kisses me deeply before slapping me on my ass.

Kane pulls our attention, "I made sure your present was in Santa's sleigh because you've been such a good girl, Eve."

My smile takes over my face, I'm so excited for all of us.

Noel has been surprisingly quiet as she watches all of us interacting with each other. When I look back at where she sits, I can see the lust in her eyes.

Breaking her silence she says, "You look good enough to eat, baby girl."

I watch as her tongue runs over her lips as she studies the three of us.

"I could say the same for you," I tell her as I pull away from Nico's embrace to join her.

After quickly shedding my clothes, I climb inside the sleigh and take a seat on the bench beside her.

Leaning into her, I whisper in her ear, "Kane fucked my ass so good last night that we had to change the bedsheet, I came so hard."

Her breath hitches as she watches the two men in front of us.

Nico has removed his clothes and is standing behind Kane. We can't see every movement but enough that we understand what they are doing.

"You see, after you wouldn't let me come," I say with a dramatic pout. "Kane had to make sure my needs were met. I told him all about what we did in the locker room, so of course he was happy to oblige."

I twirl a piece of her hair around one of my fingers. "And since he was so giving to me last night, I thought he deserved a reward."

"What's that?" She asks.

I'm more than happy to share. "Earlier, I took him into that storage closet we like so much and used my fingers to stretch his tight hole."

My lips find her neck before moving up to her mouth and kissing her. Her lips slide against mine and for a moment I savor how soft she feels.

Then I hear Kane grunt and we break apart to see what caused it.

Nico is standing behind him and his hand moves back and forth.

"After I used my fingers on him earlier, I plugged his ass. He had to work his whole shift with that between his cheeks."

Luckily, he was working security at the front entrance. Meaning any time he moved, he felt that plug inside of him.

I look at Noel with a devilish grin. "I thought maybe we could watch Nico fuck his ass tonight."

Her eyes light up with excitement just as Kane lets out a groan.

"Fuck."

Giving the guys most of my full attention, I let my hand slide over Noel's thigh. Trailing my fingers over her skin, I reach her wet center and slowly tease her.

Nico removes the plug and tosses it to the ground. He must

have rolled the condom on while we were kissing because he lines himself up and begins to slowly enter Kane.

We watch as Kane's eyes roll back in pleasure while Nico focuses on carefully pushing into him.

It's obvious when he's seated inside by the noises of pleasure they both let out.

"Fuck, that's hot."

She's watched me fuck Kane with a strap-on and knows he enjoys anal sex but to see him with another man is an entirely different experience.

It's something I want her to enjoy as well so I let my fingers get to work as she watches on, whispering dirty things quiet enough for only the two of us to hear.

"Should I have prepped you too? We could have lined you up right beside Kane and Nico could have fuck both your asses while I watched. Or maybe, I could have brought another toy with me, so that I could fuck you with it while we watched them."

Her hips thrust against my hand as I continue, putting more ideas in her head as I push two fingers inside of her while using the palm of my hand to gently circle her clit.

All of the filthy thoughts I'm giving her are ones that I'm hopeful we can find a way to accomplish in the near future.

"I'm going to come," she says as her chest rises and falls, making her breasts move up and down.

"Come all over my hand, baby. I got you." I tell her.

I look on as she meets Nico's eyes over Kane's shoulder and feel her release drench my hand. As the aftershocks run through her, she tries to pull her knees together but she's still tied up.

I'm definitely going to be cleaning this entire sleigh before we go home, starting with the bench.

Happy with myself for getting Noel off, I decide it's my turn.

Standing up, I move until my body is right in front of Noel with my back facing her face. Then, I bend over until my face is at eye level with Kane and my pussy is lined up to her mouth.

She wastes no time grabbing me by the ass and pulling me to her mouth. I'm happy that Kane only tied her legs and left her hands free.

Her tongue flattens as she licks from the top of my folds all the way back to my puckered ring before repeating the movement.

Luckily, the bench puts her at the perfect height to eat me out from behind and I can picture the way she has to be bending her body to suction her mouth around my clit.

Leaning slightly, my mouth fuses with Kane's and we kiss as Noel spears her tongue into me before sinking two fingers into me, then adding another.

It's a tight fit but feels so good, especially when her tongue begins to work around my rim. I'm coming seconds later as Kane swallows down my cries of pleasure.

Nico grunts before pistoning himself into Kane over and over, then on his final thrust, holds himself deep inside as he comes.

I'm just about to climb down to finish Kane with my mouth when Nico beats me to it. I watch in shock as our boss sinks to his knees and takes Kane's full length into his mouth.

Quickly, I move aside so that Noel can witness the scene.

Kane must be as surprised as I am because Nico only bobs his head three times before he lets out a loud moan, coming right into Nico's mouth.

Holy fuck. This might be the best sexual encounter I've ever had.

nine

KANE

I sit in a cozy little coffee shop, drinking a pumpkin spice latte, thinking about how last night will live on in my spank bank forever.

I hope that on my deathbed I'm able to recall just how good it felt to have Nico's cock inside me while I made out with Eve while she came on Noel's face.

How we were all riding the high of our orgasms as we got dressed and said goodbye before I helped Eve clean up the sleigh.

Maybe it shouldn't have felt more awkward since it's the first time that all four of us participated but it wasn't.

There was something naturally comfortable about the entire experience. And there's a possibility that last night was just the start of it all.

As long as Noel and Nico will both get on board, anyway.

When we got home last night, Eve was deliriously happy. She

69

confessed that she heard Nico and Noel in the office the day before and that's why she wanted to get us all together.

I understand it. We connect with Nico and Noel in a way that we never have with anyone else. There's a level of trust that I can feel beginning to weave into emotional intimacy. Eve said she could feel it too.

So after last night's group activities, we went home and talked through everything.

We might not have to have everything figured out right now but we do have to decide on what our next step will be. Which led me to reach out to Noel for a coffee date this morning.

I'm examining the leafy foam pattern sitting at the top of my mug when the door chimes, signaling another customer has entered.

Looking up, I see Noel wave at me before pointing to the counter.

I nod, understanding that she's going to order a drink before coming to join me. Typically, I would have waited for her before I ordered my own drink, but Noel has been touchy about me paying for her things before.

Commitment issues, they aren't easy to work around.

It's only a few minutes before she joins me, scooting into the booth seat across from me.

"What did you get?" I ask her.

Some people are judgmental about coffee orders.

But not me. I try something new on every menu, anytime I'm in a coffee shop. Today, it's the pumpkin spice latte.

And honestly? It tastes...artificial. Disappointing. Which seems ridiculous as pumpkin is an elite flavor. I guess I'll just stick to the pie.

Noel's voice knocks me out of my internal battle against the P.S.L. "'A vanilla lavender latte."

That sounds like a perfume, not a beverage.

Oh, maybe I am a judgmental coffee person. Shame. It makes sense, I had to have at least one flaw. I can't be excellent at everything.

"Did you ask me for a coffee date because of last night?" She asks.

One thing I admire about Noel is her confidence. Instead of being shy or avoiding the topic, she meets it head-on.

Shaking my head, I go with honesty, "No. Kind of."

She puts her elbows on the table and places her face in the palms of her hands with an amused look on her face. "Well, I'm all ears."

This feels scarier than it did ten minutes ago but I'm not going to hold back. If she rejects us, that's her right.

"I know you have a couple of days off from work," I start. "Do you think that maybe while you're away, you could be thinking about the future?"

"It might be hard to believe, Kane," she says with a tilt of her head, "I've been thinking about the future a lot lately."

With an encouraging smile, I nod for her to continue.

Noel takes a sip of her latte before looking at me thoughtfully. "I am ready to make some changes. It's something I've been considering for a while but recent events have helped me find some clarity.

"Clarity is good," I tell her as I reach for her hand, wanting to be as supportive as I can be.

"My roommate is moving out to live with her boyfriends. She doesn't stay at our apartment much anyway but we've lived together for pretty much our entire adult lives. It got me thinking about how empty my place feels."

Pulling away from me, she sits back in her booth and I give her the time she needs to figure out what she wants to say next.

"I don't know, Kane. I'm starting to realize it's not just the apartment that's empty. I feel empty too."

She looks so damn sad when she says it and it makes me want to scoop her up and hold her but I hesitate.

Noel just said she feels empty though. So I climb out of my seat and move into hers, pulling her into me.

"It's okay. We'll figure everything out." I don't think much about my wording but she catches it.

"We?"

I look down to where her head is resting on my shoulder. "Yeah, we. If you wanted us to, Noel. We'd be there for you anytime you needed. I really mean that."

She lifts her head to study my face. I'm not sure what she finds but she rests her head again after a few seconds.

"I believe you, Kane. I feel like my whole world might change soon. I want to find something more stable that can make me happy while making enough money to live comfortably on my own."

Noel's definitely been thinking about things. I'm shocked to hear she might leave SantaScape.

"The downfall of adulting, I guess," I say sympathetically.

She lets out a quiet laugh. "Earlier this week, I thought it was the end of the world. As much as I hate to admit it, I was scared. All of these changes and decisions have been overwhelming."

I can only imagine how it would feel to not only have your work life change drastically but to also have major changes at home.

"It has to be tough but it sounds like you are being pretty strong through it all. The way you told off Nico was fucking hot." I do my best to give her a playful smolder, trying to keep the conversation as light as possible.

Noel gives me a smug smirk, "He deserved it."

He did. Someone had to give Nico a little bit of a fight. We've never really sat down and had a full-on conversation about his work. I can't help but think that something is weighing down on him.

"I don't disagree with you but I'm wondering if there's a bigger picture at play. Companies don't make a bunch of budget cuts as quickly as Nico did for no reason."

Eve hasn't mentioned anything specific but I know she's seen the signs too.

Noel looks contemplative as if she didn't consider that there could be something more going on.

"Maybe it's nothing but I wanted to point out that we don't always know why someone is making their decisions," I say, making sure my tone isn't condescending.

"And maybe I wanted to help humanize our office Grinch too."

That earns me another laugh and the sound filters through my ears and settles in my chest with pride.

She rolls her eyes at me. "I don't *really* hate him, you know? He was just so damn...bossy."

I chuckle. "That is kind of his job."

We settle into a brief, comfortable silence for a few moments before I make a move.

"With all of those changes in your life, would one more be too much?"

Her eyes sparkle with interest. "I guess that depends on what it is."

I turn in the booth so we're face to face but keep her hands cupped in mine. "Give us a real chance."

Her teeth bite down on her lips nervously. "You mean...like an exclusive relationship?"

"Yes. The four of us." Making it clear that we want her and Nico.

"Nico, too?" She asks.

"I'm talking to you first, one one-on-one, because we didn't want to overwhelm or scare you. We've thought about it a lot and this isn't the first time we've wanted to try to have a real relationship with you. But joining a couple with as much history as Eve and I, we thought it might be too much."

Any relationship is going to have challenges but with more people to consider, those challenges can be even harder to overcome. I think we can handle it.

"Is Eve going to talk to Nico, too?"

I nod in confirmation. "We want you both onboard but you should know that even if he says no, it's not going to change how we feel about you or what we want."

I mean every word I say.

Noel should be with us and if she says no today, we'll wait until she's ready. But we're done searching for something that we've already found.

"Take the next couple of days to think about it. Do whatever you need to do. We'll be waiting whenever you're ready to talk and we'll continue to care about you no matter what you decide."

I kiss her on the top of her head before leaving her in the booth.

On my way out of the coffee shop, I let the nerves I've been hiding rise to the surface. I really hope they both want this too.

ten

*H*aving a couple of days off was exactly what I needed to clear my mind. After my conversation with Kane, I had a lot to think about.

His offer to join them, and possibly Nico, was enticing.

My first instinct was to chase Kane out of that coffee shop and tell him yes. But he was right. I needed to think it through.

I had to make sure that I wasn't making a rash decision just because I've started feeling so lost and lonely. I care about each of them but I won't deny that the idea of closing our dynamic off felt like things got very serious, very fast.

It's not that I'm against relationships. I've just never been in one. Or wanted to be.

My feelings for Eve and Kane have always been there, even if I refused to admit it. And when I let go of my anger for Nico's decisions and took time to consider that he could be coming from a good place, I know that I could easily develop those same feelings for him.

I can't deny that starting a relationship with not one person, but three, feels like I'm jumping into the deep end of the pool without any arm floats. Ultimately though, my feelings for them have easily outweighed my nerves, and I'm ready to be honest with them about that.

And I know just where I need to start.

The boss.

I have no idea how his conversation may have gone with Eve but we can't let those two, even with their good intentions, run this entire thing for us. He and I are going to have to work on our own relationship.

In order to prove that I'm ready for this, I think it's best if I talk with Nico first. I want to know where he stands and if all of this is just fun and games.

Because if he's not in this, can we really move on as just a throuple? I know Eve and Kane believe that they want me no matter what, but what if we try it and they feel like he's really their missing piece.

My steps are confident as I make my way down the hall, approaching Nico's office.

Eve isn't at her desk, which doesn't strike me as odd. Although she takes her work seriously and is good at her job, I know first hand that she's a coffee fiend with a habit of office hookups.

She could be in Nico's office with him but I'm certain that pending a work emergency, she'd let me have a private conversation with him.

Or at least pretend to while she listened at the door.

I'm about to know when I notice a slight crack. Peeking

through, I realize that Nico is definitely in his office alone, pacing the room.

"I understand that but if we could just have a little more time..." He sounds frustrated.

I'm about to give him a signal that I'm here but the conversation seems to escalate quickly.

"That's just it, Jack. I'm doing everything I can to make sure this place survives while you're out on a private island relaxing."

Survives? Maybe Kane was onto something. Nico might be making all of these changes and canceling our big celebration to save the company money.

It sounds like that's true but that it might be a much bigger deal than a few budget cuts.

"No, Jack. I'm saying you won't even have a job when you get back to the states. SantaScape is going to have to close its doors after this season."

The finality of his words cause me to let out a gasp loud enough that Nico stops and turns. I'm in shock. Suspecting something and having it confirmed are very different things.

Opening the door fully, I narrow my eyes at him. "What is going on, Nico?"

He sighs, "Jack, I'll call you back." Without waiting for a response, he puts the phone away. "How much did you hear, Noel?"

It's interesting to me that he doesn't try to make an immediate excuse or brush me off. Even though he's been caught, he could easily tell me to leave and mind my own business.

Nico doesn't though. Instead, I watch his shoulders fall in shame.

"I'm going to be real with you, Noel. My uncle left this place dangling above the red. I've made all the cuts I can to the budget but I don't think we're going to make it."

I nod. That, I can understand. We're a seasonal business focused on one holiday celebration. It wouldn't take a business expert to know it's a risk.

"And the other thing? About Jack?" I ask as I take a few steps towards him.

Nico runs a hand through his hair. "I'm supposed to be done at the end of the year."

I inhale and exhale, willing some of my anger to leave my body. My plan was to enter this room and have a conversation about our future. Instead, I'm learning that maybe there was never meant to be a future for us at all.

"When were you going to tell us, Nico? All of us depend on this job in some way." It occurs to me as I'm speaking that maybe not all of us were in the dark.

Eve and Kane have been close with Nico much longer than I have. Did they know this was possible?

"I didn't want anyone to know, Noel. I was hoping to find a way to fix this before it ever got to this point."

And maybe if that were the only problem here, I could easily move past it. But he's also planning to leave us and didn't say anything about it.

"Was this job always temporary? Why didn't you tell us that?" For as many of those stupid memos he sent out, one of them could have included this information.

He looks at me like I'm silly for asking. "You and everyone else here wouldn't have respected me or the changes that had to be made if you thought this was all temporary. It was my uncle's idea."

I hate that he's right. I never would have abided by any rules he set because I would have assumed they'd change again the moment he left.

"Maybe. But that doesn't change the fact that you didn't tell me sooner. Or Kane and Eve."

"Tell us what?" Kane's voice startles me from where he stands behind me in the doorway.

He and Eve are holding coffee cups and pastries, something I imagine they thought the four of us would be sharing.

"That he's leaving. That SantaScape is failing financially and he never planned to be here long enough to see the dust settle after it all crumbles." I paint the picture exactly as it looks in my mind.

Eve sets the items in her hands down on Nico's desk before making her way beside me, grabbing my hand as she looks at Nico with betrayal on her face.

I guess she really didn't know either. Which means whatever conversation they had the other day, he didn't even give her the courtesy of telling her the truth.

Kane leans against the wall, drinking a cup of coffee that is probably full of sugar and cream and little caffeine. He looks casual but his shoulders are hunched enough to give him away. "Is that true, Nico?"

Nico rounds his desk and collapses in his chair. "That's not how I was going to break it to everyone, but yes."

"How else is there to say it? How did you plan to sugarcoat your leaving to the three people you've been fucking?" I say with anger biting through my voice.

He groans. "It wasn't like that. You all knew my uncle was retiring and someone was supposed to take over. It was going to be my cousin, Jack, but he had some problem over Halloween weekend that led to him needing to wait until the new year."

Eve tries to lead me to take a seat on the couch but I don't feel like sitting. That seems like a calm reaction and I definitely am not feeling calm.

"So they called and asked if I would fill in until he could get here. My uncle didn't let me in on just how much trouble he was in until I got here and I suspect he thought with my skillset that I could fix it. But I don't know if I can."

His voice is filled with defeat as he says "Then I met Eve...and Kane...and you, Noel. I thought we'd all have some fun and..."

"And then you'd leave." Eve is the one to say it.

I'm glad it wasn't me because the words send a jolt of pain through my chest. I'm no stranger to casual hookups and fun times but the other night felt different.

They made it seem like it was different.

Nico speaks up again, "At first, yes. That's exactly what I planned to do. Now, though, things are different. We talked and I want this, we can figure it out."

I'm over this conversation. I need to leave. I need to run away and never come back here. "Well, it doesn't have to be different. This was fun and all, but I'll see you around. Or not. Whatever."

I realize I'm being an asshole to Eve and Kane who don't deserve it but I need to protect the slice of my heart I was willing to give to this arrangement before it shatters even more.

"Don't leave this way, Noel." Kane pleads as he tries to block the door.

"Let me go, Kane." I hold back the tears in my eyes but I know he can see them. "Please," I beg.

Slowly, he slides out of my path and I take the opportunity to run.

eleven

EVE

$\mathcal{N}$ico has us all in a really shitty situation.

First, he withheld the full truth of what he was here for. Second, he said he wanted a relationship but fucked it up before we even started.

When we sat down and talked the other day, he said he wanted this, wanted us. He was genuine and excited even though he was nervous about how Noel was going to feel about it.

He's asked me three times a day if she's called and each time I've told him to be patient. So he'd return to his office, obsessing over his notebook. I've heard that thing slam on the desk several times.

Of course, Noel shows up today and he blew it straight to the south pole. I'm guessing so anyway, I don't think she would have reacted with so much anger and disappointment if she hadn't been here to say yes.

But now we don't know what she was thinking and we're all in a mess.

Now, I'm going to fucking fix it.

I point my finger at him with a scowl on my face, "I'm mad at you. Really, really mad. But I am choosing to believe that you did mean it when you told me that you wanted this realtionship to work with the four of us."

Kane gives Nico a warning look, conveying just how much trouble he's in, but it goes ignored.

"What do I do now?" Nico asks solemnly.

My hands find my way to their hips as I stare at him. "You should probably tell us everything. I can't fix a problem if I don't know just how bad it is."

Nico moves over to his bottom drawer and pulls out a notebook. "The business isn't able to continue if we continue to be a one holiday operation. We need to add another stream of revenue to keep a profit because SantaScape is barely paying for itself."

Kane and I sit in the chairs across from Nico's desk and listen intently.

"I have a few ideas but these aren't going to be short term solutions. The ideas that I think are worth trying are long games."

Nodding, I motion for him to continue.

"It doesn't make sense that we have some of the most extravagant, yet beautiful, holiday decor in the world but we only display it."

"You want us to sell it?" I ask, catching on to it.

Kane shakes his head. "Wouldn't we need a manufacturer? And investors?"

Nico nods.

"I hate to be a negative nelly," I say. "But isn't the market a little oversaturated with Christmas decor?"

We might be belle of the Christmas ball but people aren't always willing to pay for something when they can find a duplicate product for cheaper, even if it means sacrificing quality.

"That's why we need an edge. We need to invest in more than Christmas decor and open it up to a diverse selection of celebrations, bringing qualified individuals who understand them along with artists who can find the right vision."

Nico's voice is filled with passion as he explains this. This must be what he's been working on for the last two days.

"It's not good enough though. We need to find something that sets us apart from your normal home decor corporations and pop-up shops."

That's when the light bulb comes on for me and I run out to my desk. I flip through my contacts until I find the right number and phone in a favor.

It only takes a few minutes, and a name drop that could get me in trouble, but this might be worth it.

"We have to go," I tell the two men watching as I grab my coat. "We have a meeting in an hour and we cannot be late. Bring the notebook."

They follow the order without question, though I'm sure they will have plenty on the car ride.

Let's just hope we can pull off a Christmas miracle.

WE'RE SITTING in a conference room at the Ground Up headquarters waiting for our meeting to begin when I start to question whether or not I should have called Noel for this.

I don't have time to dwell before her best friend enters the room with two men.

"Eve!" She says as she comes over to where I'm sitting and I stand to meet her hug. "It's been too long since our last girl's night. We should put one on the calendar soon."

I smile when both of the men groan at the idea. Maybe because they don't want to spend a night away from her or maybe because our girl's nights never stay as chill as we promise. I've only been around for two of them and I woke up the next morning smelling like a distillery.

We all take our seats, with the Ground Up team sitting across from us.

"This is Romeo and Beau," she says as she gestures to each man.

I won't lie, these men are attractive. But I think my guys might be a little hotter.

"Kane and Nicholas," I introduce my own team.

Val giggles. "Oh, yes, I guess I'm not entitled to the privilege of calling you Nico."

I swear I see a blush on his cheeks and I wonder exactly why she would have said that. And why he would have reacted.

It must be because of something that Noel told her.

"I really appreciate you taking the time to meet us at the last minute, Val." I tell her genuinely.

She waves her hand. "Of course. I'm sorry Hart couldn't make it, he had a prior appointment."

I nod in understanding. "We wanted to talk over a business opportunity with you. And before we give you our pitch please know I would never have put you in this position if we weren't desperate."

Val nods, "it sounds serious. What's going on?"

Nico pulls out his folder and begins talking through the same idea he pitched to us back at SantaScape.

"This sounds interesting but can I ask why you thought we were the people to bring this to?" Beau asks. He's not rude, just confused.

Nico gestures for me to take over.

"We understand that right now, this sounds like a supermarket holiday aisle idea. We thought so too," I say with a playful smile. "I thought we should bring it to your team because of your sustainability efforts."

Val's eyes light up before she shares a sly smile with her partners. "You want to make an eco-friendly line of diverse holiday decor."

"Exactly," I tell her. I'm impressed with how quickly she caught on.

Romeo's face is full of curiosity. "And how fast are you hoping to move this process."

Nico speaks up, "As fast as we can."

I watch as Val looks at both of her partners, sharing looks that must be communicating without vocalizing any words.

Meeting my eyes, Val smiles. "We're interested. It aligns with an initiative of mine and I think that if we were to work together, with the right team, this could be something incredible."

"But," Kane asks.

I tap his knee with my open hand, trying to scold him without them noticing.

"But we need to pitch it to Hart, too," Val says kindly.

I see Romeo and Beau look over her head to share matching grins. Something tells me that Hart doesn't often say no to Val.

Reaching across the table, I shake each of their hands before Kane does the same.

"One more thing, if you wouldn't mind," Nico says and we all take our seats again. "I have a really big favor to ask and it's not an easy one."

He explains his idea and I absolutely adore it.

So does Val.

I just hope it works.

twelve

NOEL

$\mathcal{A}$fter leaving Nico's office, I was upset.

I wanted to call Val and ask her to meet me at the apartment with a bottle of vodka and I almost did. Then I thought about how before I overheard Nico, I planned to take the necessary steps to move forward with my life in a more serious manner. The first was to try my hand at a relationship with three other people.

That might be on hold for now but there were other things I could do to start my journey.

So I called Val anyway. I asked if she could meet me at the apartment. She said she would as soon as she got out of an important meeting.

I'm waiting outside the apartment leasing office for her now, thinking about how easy it felt to not chase my sadness with anger.

I'll still be having vodka later because I'm still really fucking mad. But I can be a grown-up first.

Val runs up the sidewalk and hugs me tight.

"Are you okay?" I ask.

She's very energetic, practically jumping in place. "Me? I'm wonderful. What are we doing here though?" Her tone turns suspicious. "Wait is there someone waiting in there to hold me hostage so that I have to extend the lease and stay in our apartment with you for the next fifty years?"

I laugh so hard I have to bend over, completely out of breath.

We both know that I would pull something like that.

"It's the opposite. I'm trying to grow up." I tell her.

Val's face drops and I'm surprised. I've put her through some wild things over the years and I thought she'd be relieved.

"Noel, you are perfect. You're a majestic unicorn in a world of darkness." She tells me while pulling me in for a hug. "Please don't change that."

My eyes water up. "It's okay, Val. I'm still going to make you go out for girls' night just to end up at a tattoo parlor while we wait for your guys to come and stop us."

It's happened three times in the last six months. I can't help it, drunk Val is always convinced she wants some ink and I enjoy the way Hart stares at all the male tattoo artists who could have tried to touch her.

"What's this growing-up nonsense?" She asks, pulling away and putting her hands on her hips.

I shrug, feeling eerily calm. "I'm ready to make some changes. I was even thinking about trying my hand at relationships and careers but I thought we could start with something small."

She raises her left brow curiously. "And that would be?"

My arm winds through hers, leading the way into the building. "Getting my own lease."

A kind lady takes us to her desk and begins explaining our options.

Assuming I'd need to find a smaller place that I could afford on my own, I was prepared for us to both move out of our apartment. Then Val pulled out her checkbook and paid twelve months' rent to ensure that I could keep our place for another year.

When I asked her why, she said it was a Christmas present from her and the guys, but mostly the guys. It's annoying that they love her so much that they'd do something so nice for her best friend. It's a little hard to be mad at them for stealing her way now.

The paperwork takes no time at all and within an hour, we're sitting at a bar down the street, celebrating our new living statuses.

"Now, spill, what encouraged this new journey of maturity," Val asks.

Rolling my eyes, I sip my drink slowly before I answer. "After you told me that you were moving out, I decided I wanted to make some changes."

"Making some changes would be turning my room into a home gym or adding a sex swing in the living room. You said career and relationship. Those are not even in the same ballpark, my friend."

Val looks smug, as if she believes she's caught me in a trap.

"Okay well, first of all, a gym is for people who don't puke at the thought of cardio," I tell her with my nose wrinkled in disgust. "Second of all, I...might have started fooling around with Eve and Kane again."

Val squeals. "And?"

"I like them. They're fun and thoughtful and I've always felt safe with them."

"What are you leaving out?" Her eyes narrow.

Grinning, I wiggle my brows up and down. "That Nico also bent me over his desk and gave me a spanking. Then I watched him fuck Kane while eating Eve's pussy in Santa's sleigh."

Luckily, Val turns her head in time to not spray me with her drink. "Holy shit."

If I look smug, it's because I am.

"So is that why you mentioned a relationship?"

I catch her up to speed on everything. Val is sympathetic and understanding, even when she tries to add reason to a situation I'm not quite willing to focus on resolving right now.

When we've finished a second round of drinks, we close our bar tab and part with a hug.

She leaves to be with her guys and I feel a sense of longing. This morning, I thought I would be on my way to something special like that.

I'm disappointed that today didn't turn out how I expected but I'm also grateful that at least one part of my future doesn't look so uncertain.

When I walk through the apartment door, I'm expecting to feel something. Instead, I still feel empty. I can't help but wonder what it'd be like to call Eve and see if she wants to come over and eat a gallon of ice cream with me. Or to ask Kane if he wants to hang out on the couch and watch a movie.

And Nico. Maybe I could learn what he likes to do for fun too.

But for now, I'm going to keep taking my baby steps. I have time to figure out the rest.

thirteen

NICO

*I*t's been one week. Seven days.

And I haven't gotten to say one word to Noel.

Besides Kane and Eve, we've all been giving each other space.

We've had a couple of meetings with the team at GroundUp, starting to put things in motion on the new project. I've enjoyed seeing the beginning stages.

I was shocked when Hart suggested that I should consider coming on board as an analyst for the project. He said my skills would be better put to use collecting data and using it to help ensure each stage of the process flows as smoothly as possible.

After he put the idea in my head, it's been all I can think about. I finally feel like I might have a job where I'm happy with what I do again. Plus, I wouldn't have to leave SantaScape.

I haven't given him an answer yet. There are a few things I need to take care of before I can make my decision.

Christmas is days away and it's not even close to being the happiest time of the year for me.

I miss them. All of them. I'm tired of the space between us.

That should change any minute now.

No sooner than the thought crosses my mind, there's banging at my office door.

"Come in," I say as I lean back in my chair and throw my feet up on the desk attempting to look relaxed.

Noel bursts through my door and I almost flinch from the bang it makes against the wall.

"Is this a joke?" She's holding up what I believe is my most recent employee memo.

I shake my head disapprovingly. "Work is nothing to joke about, little elf."

She narrows her eyes at my name for her. "Don't call me that. And who do you think you are? A mandatory staff meeting? And you're closing the place down early?"

I nod, acting as casually as I can. "I believe you understand the message. If that's all, you really should be getting ready for your shift."

Her eyes widen in anger as she throws her hands up. "Unbelievable. I thought you were Scrooge before. Now, I'm questioning if you're Krampus."

A demon. She's calling me the demon of Christmas. I can't help but chuckle as I remove my feet from the desk and stand, approaching her.

Gently, I guide her with an arm around her shoulders back to the door. "Mandatory means not optional, little elf. Now get to work."

I close the door behind her and smile. Tonight will be fun.

———

"Alright, boss. Everything is in place." Kane tells me.

I'm standing in the middle of our largest conference room, observing all the finishing touches. It's the same room that I stood in not too long ago as my uncle announced I'd be taking over for him.

Now, it's a symbol of the future of SantaScape.

I look at Kane with a smile. "Thanks for all your help."

"No problem. This place looks really fucking cool. Getting some prototype rush ordered was a great idea, Nico. And the displays with all the ideas for the first launch turned out awesome."

"I couldn't agree more," I say as I reach my hands up to grip each side of his face before kissing him.

His mouth is rough, and his lips even feel a little dry, but they move against mine with fevered need. When we break apart, he's staring at me in shock.

"What was that for?"

"Because I miss you. And I'm done waiting. Tonight, you're all coming home with me." I wink as I walk away.

There are only a few more minutes before the employees should start filtering into the room and I want to watch their reactions.

I find a seat near the podium just as the DJ starts up the playlist.

Absurd remixes of classic holiday songs begin to fill the air as the doors open and bodies start to enter.

Their faces are filled with mixes of confusion and appreciation. Interest and awe.

The moment Noel enters the room, her eyes meet mine. The annoyance quickly fades away from her features as she wanders around the displays.

When I'm sure everyone is here, I signal for the DJ to fade the music out before stepping up to the podium.

I'm surprisingly nervous for as confident and excited as I've felt all day. I clear my throat before speaking.

"If I could have your attention for a moment, please." The room quiets as my voice rings out across the room. "You might be wondering why I've forced you all to be here."

There are a few nods of acknowledgment.

"Recently, I've had to make some tough choices in my role as your leader. I didn't necessarily want to but I did what I thought was best for the company."

I let that resonate in the room before continuing.

"I should have realized what my uncle did in all his years here. That you, the employees, are the best thing for the company. Some of you are working here as a second job or just for fun. Some of you have spent many holiday seasons with us. All of you are valuable and crucial to our goal of keeping SantaScape the best place for holiday entertainment."

There are some eye rolls, people who don't care for the praise I'm giving. Others are holding on for what I'm going to say next.

"That said, I need to be honest with you. SantaScape was in a worrisome position financially at the start of this season. I didn't see how we were going to make it. So I started making cuts. If I'm honest, I was struggling with what I could do to help and I took the easiest route I could."

I don't like admitting faults, I imagine most people don't but accountability is important.

"I'm happy to tell you that there will be more changes in the future and before anyone starts booing me," I look straight into Noel's eyes and she shrugs as if she might behave but could just as easily entice a riot.

"In the New Year, SantaScape will be re-organizing and re-branding. The displays you see around the room are just a few examples of our plans and the beautiful decorations around the room are courtesy prototypes from our partners in this initiative, Ground Up. We look forward to connecting with them to become the most sustainable and diverse holiday decor brand while continuing to provide our seasonal entertainment."

A round of applause goes off throughout the room.

"Appetizers, pizza, and drinks will be available for the next hour. I hope you enjoy this small token of my appreciation for all you do."

I might have caved on the pizza party but at least I was nice enough to serve it in addition to decent food.

I step down from the podium and walk through the room.

The hour passes by quickly and before I know it, the last of the employees are leaving for the night.

"That was impressive, Nico," Eve tells me as she kisses my cheek.

I pull her in for a real kiss before saying, "It couldn't have happened without you. Reaching out to Ground Up was brilliant."

A slow clap starts nearby and I look over to see Noel watching us with a smile on her face. Kane is standing right beside her, looking giddy.

Noel speaks first, "Should we visit the sleigh again? Or maybe Rudolph's house."

"As interesting as that sounds," I say. "The three of you are coming home with me tonight."

We all exchange excited glances and I'm about ready to leave. There's just one last thing I've been wanting to take care of.

Closing the space between us, I reach for the back of Noel's head and bring our mouths together. I groan when her tongue pushes past my lips.

Breaking away, I toss her over my shoulder before reaching for my keys and walking towards the exit.

"Get your things and meet me out front," I tell the other two.

The cleaning crew will be here any minute and I want to be out of the building before they arrive.

I meant it when I said I was tired of waiting.

Tonight, they're all mine.

fourteen

We burst into Nico's bedroom in a frenzy, the four of us tearing pieces of clothing off each other until we're all naked.

"How do you want to start this?" I ask them.

"What about a classic sixty-nine?" Noel has barely finished her sentence before I'm lifting her and throwing her over me on the bed.

My face is buried in her cunt less than a second later and I feel Eve and Nico join us on the bed. Noel wraps her lips around my cock and I reward her by latching onto her clit.

I should have had her ride my face first so I could really concentrate on making her come. Instead, I'm battling against her talented mouth.

I lick her from the top of her slit to her entrance before spearing my tongue inside her as she uses one hand to grip my balls while taking me down her throat as far as she can.

Eve's moans tell me that Nico is taking good care of her but I'm selfish and want a taste of them, too.

I pull away from Noel and say, "Spit on that sweet pussy, Nico, and then switch me. I want to taste all of you together."

I follow my own instruction and we all maneuver until Eve is riding my face while trying to choke on my dick. I try and tunnel my tongue inside her, wanting to dig out the taste of Nico too.

Noel must have done something to drive Nico crazy because one second he's growling into her cunt and the next he's got her flipped onto her back while he lines up with her entrance and thrusts inside.

"Yes, Nico, fuck."

Her head is beside mine on the bed and she watches me lick Eve's pussy like she wishes she could lean up and help.

She could probably try if Nico wasn't holding her down with his hand on her throat.

Eve turns around and lines me up with her own entrance before sinking down on me. She's practically dripping as she uses me like a fuck toy, riding me while leaning over to bite down on Nico's shoulder.

He lets go of Noel's throat so he can grab Eve's instead, pulling her mouth to his and biting down on her lower lip, returning the pain.

The action causes her to gush on me and I reach up to pinch both of her nipples. That sends her over the edge and she squeezes me so tight that I almost follow her.

Instead, I wait until Nico's no longer holding her to flip her under me, with her stomach on the bed. I move her until she can hover her face over Noel's before I start fucking her from behind.

We all look so good together. Noel lying under Eve while Nico thrusts into her wildly.

Noel's mouth comes up to lick at my balls before moving away. Judging by the noise that leaves Eve's lips, she must be alternating her attention between my balls and Eve's clit.

Eve leans down to return the attention and my nails dig into her ass at the sight of her suctioning her mouth to Noel's center.

This sends her over the edge and her pussy squeezes me tightly.

Nico isn't far behind, letting go inside Noel after a few more thrusts.

That just leaves me.

I pull out of Eve and stand up from the bed, holding my cock out to both women.

"Suck."

They follow the order and take turns taking me to the back of their throats.

Eve leans down to suck my balls into her mouth while Noel swallows around my dick. It doesn't take long before I can feel the pressure of an orgasm building in my spine.

Somehow, Nico manages to sneak behind me. His finger starts to circle my asshole and I know I'm going to lose it.

"Let me paint your tits with my cum."

Both girls position themselves while Nico uses his free hand to grab hold of my cock and finishes me off, rubbing my release over both sets of beautiful breasts.

Once every drop has marked them, I watch as they take turns cleaning it off one another. Taking their time to suck on the other's nipples and leaving no trace of me on their skin.

What a Merry fucking Christmas.

epilogue

NOEL

*C*hristmas morning, I wake up surrounded by body heat. The four of us have somehow entangled ourselves in a way that everyone is touching each other.

For a few moments, I enjoy the quiet room and appreciate not waking up alone on a holiday. After Nico's party for the staff where he pitched the company's new direction, things have continued to get better.

Including the four of us officially becoming an exclusive group.

Sure, our relationship might look strange to the outside world, but I've never really cared about what people think anyway. So whatever people have to say, bring it on.

It's going to be really interesting with all of us still working together since Nico has decided to come on board as the company's project analyst since Jack is taking over as CEO in January.

113

Eve is going to move to the new department and remain Nico's secretary.

Kane and I plan to return as seasonal employees next holiday season but he will also be helping build the new sales platform.

As for me, I've been shadowing all of them, trying to get a feel for what I might like to try. Nico and Val both suggested I help with the selection process for the designers and it sounds like fun. Maybe I can put all my wild energy into a form of creative outlet.

"What has that smile on your face this morning?" Nico asks quietly as he lifts himself out of bed.

I roll out from Kane's leg hold and follow him to the kitchen. "I was just thinking that it's nice to not be alone this morning."

Nico comes up behind me and cages me in his arms against the counter while I begin to brew a pot of coffee.

His house is beautiful. Not extravagant but a definite upgrade from my apartment. Plus, he has the biggest bed.

He nuzzles his nose against my neck, "I like not waking up alone on Christmas either."

I tilt my neck, granting him more access.

"As much as I want to bend you over this counter and fuck you so hard that you can't walk straight, I know for a fact that you have a surprise waiting."

I turn around in his embrace and rest my arms on his shoulders. "If I didn't love surprises so much, I just might let you."

Another voice joins us. "Well, surprise!"

Turning to face Kane, I can't help the laughter that belts out of me.

At first, it looks like he's holding a present. But he isn't.

He's *wearing* a present. Over his dick. He put his dick in a gift box. And the only possible way that could stay is if he's fully erect.

My eyes are watering from how hard I'm laughing.

Eve walks into the room, making a show out of wiping the corner of her mouth. "You're welcome."

She sucked his dick, not to completion, so that he could put it in a box. For me.

This is a perfect gift for me and the fact that it was a group effort is kind of sweet.

I walk towards Kane, dropping my robe as I do. "Should I open that now? Or wait?"

"Now, please. Do you know how many elderly nutsacks I had to imagine so I wouldn't blow my load down Eve's throat?" Kane says with a disturbed look on his face.

"Well thank goodness for old man balls," Nico says deadpan.

This entire situation is ridiculous. I love it.

Before I can sink to my knees, Eve is there, laying down a pillow. She winks before heading into the kitchen and kissing Nico.

Gently, I pull the box off of Kane, only to reveal a cock ring that immediately begins to vibrate.

I look back at Eve who is holding the remote with a devilish grin on her face.

Kane groans. "Fuck, I'm not gonna last. Maybe you should just ride me and skip the blow job."

Nico laughs, "Skip the blow job? Listen to you, you're losing it. Pull it together, Kane."

The vibration seems to settle into a low hum, meaning Eve is showing him a little mercy.

Before he can protest again, I take him all the way to the back of my throat until my nose is pressed against his abdomen.

"Oh, fuck. Noel. You feel so fucking good." His words come out rushed.

Slowly, I back off before repeating the action. His hands come up and grab the back of my head, holding me in place.

"Fuck, I wish I could just hold my dick down your throat. I'd keep it there all fucking day if I could. Sit on the couch with my cock in your mouth and put on a movie."

We should do that one day, when my mouth isn't full of dick I'll be sure to put in an official request to be used as his personal cock warmer.

The sound of Nico's thrusts meeting Eve's ass with a slapping noise ring out through the kitchen. I'm not the least bit jealous that he's doing to her what he just told me he wanted to do to me. I know I'll be the one to soothe her wrecked pussy in the bathtub later.

I continue to deep-throat Kane until he can't take it, lifting me until I'm in his arms.

He carries me to the couch before sitting down with me straddling him. His fingers slide down my center to make sure I'm ready before lifting my hips and seating me on his cock.

"Ride me, Noel. Fucking ride me."

As soon as he's inside me, the vibration is intensified and we're both moaning.

I look up to see Eve drop the remote as Nico slams into her over and over. He has one hand on a hip and the other gripping her hair. One of her legs is resting against the height of the counter as she takes him.

It's a beautiful scene. Every single time we do something like this, it gets hotter.

I start to pick up my pace, trying to match the rhythm of Eve and Nico, riding Kane hard like he wanted.

He groans and I lean down to bite his earlobe before saying, "That's it, take my pussy like a good boy, Kane."

I can feel my orgasm building and I look back to the kitchen, making eye contact with Eve. Her mouth opens in a silent scream just as I do the same.

Nico groans, signaling that he's reached his end too.

Kane grabs hold of my hips and starts thrusting up into me, taking control, and bringing on an orgasm that has the corners of my vision darkening.

I have a feeling that two orgasms are just the beginning of our holiday celebration.

acknowledgments

Wow!

I hope you enjoyed Noel's story. In the words of the great Taylor Swift, it's been a long time coming.

Thank you so much for picking up this story. It was really fun to write and I can't help but wonder if this world or it's characters have more to offer.

Now, to the praise...

Cassie. You my boy, blue. If you didn't encourage my terrible habits, this book would not be finished.

Kris and Kate. You bitches light up my life.

Jess, you're precious and I appreciate that you don't get mad when I stop responding because I'm trying to pretend that I'm responsible.

Claudia, thanks for fueling my coffee addiction.

My baby girlfriend Anna, because even if we never finalize a plan for brunch, I like that we text about it a lot.

Tricia, my main one.

Aley, my day one.

My family for making sure I have the time and resources to write.

And to Cadbury. Without the ability to reward myself with Carmello Koalas and Wallabys, I would have greatly suffered.

Last but not least, my readers. Particularly the ones who hyped me up to write a book with FF. The people who hop in my DMs and share my posts.

I fucking love you.

about the author

Drea Denae is a romance author living in Texas with her husband, daughter and four dogs. She prefers coffee and the brief fall weather. Drea likes to coach her daughter's sports teams, even though she usually has no idea what she is doing. When she isn't writing, she likes to read all kinds of stories that reflect the real world we live in, even if weaved into a fictional story line.

instagram.com/authordreadenae
tiktok.com/@authordreadenae
threads.net/@authordreadenae

also by drea denae

Caged In Flames

Burn It Down

Cupid Is A C*nt

(Holiday Hoemies Book 1)

Made in the USA
Coppell, TX
22 November 2024

40804487R00074